THE WHEELS
The Friendship Race

바퀴 달린 친구들
친구들과의 경주

Inna Nusinsky
저자 이나 누진스키

Illustrations by Michael Jay Roque
그림 마이클 제이 로크

www.kidkiddos.com

Copyright©2015 by S. A. Publishing ©2017 by KidKiddos Books Ltd.

support@kidkiddos.com

All rights reserved. No part of this book may be reproduced in any form or by any electronic or mechanical means, including information storage and retrieval systems, without written permission from the publisher or author, except in the case of a reviewer, who may quote brief passages embodied in critical articles or in a review.

모든 권한을 보유합니다.

First edition, 2017

Translated from English by Tay Bake

영한 옮김 백태은

Korean editing by Jiwon Ahn

번역 감수 안지원

The Wheels: The Friendship race (Korean Bilingual Edition)
ISBN: 978-1-5259-0480-6 paperback
ISBN: 978-1-5259-0481-3 hardcover
ISBN: 978-1-5259-0479-0 eBook

Although the author and the publisher have made every effort to ensure the accuracy and completeness of information contained in this book, we assume no responsibility for errors, inaccuracies, omission, inconsistency, or consequences from such information.

Please note that the Korean and English versions of the story have been written to be as close as possible. However, in some cases they differ in order to accommodate nuances and fluidity of each language.

Jonny the car looked at himself in the shop window. How handsome he was! And what speed – he could beat even race cars!

자동차 조니는 가게 창문에 비친 자기 모습을 바라보고 있었어요. 정말 잘생긴 얼굴이지요! 속도도 엄청 빠르구요 - 레이싱 자동차도 이길 수 있었으니까요!

"I'm the pride of the neighborhood," he yelled.
"내가 우리 동네에서 제일 멋져," 조니가 말했어요.

Just then, two braking sounds broke his daydream.

바로 그 때, 두 개의 브레이크 밟는 소리가 조니의 달콤한 공상을 깨뜨렸어요.

There were his friends: Mike the bike and Scott the scooter.

그건 바로 조니의 친구들이었어요: 자전거 마이크와 킥보드 스캇이었죠.

"Hey Jonny!" his friends said. "What's up?"

"안녕 조니!" 친구들이 인사했어요. "뭐하고 있었니?"

"Feeling like a little race today," said Jonny, puffing his tires. "But there's no one I can race with."

"오늘 경주나 나가볼까 생각 중이었지," 조니가 붕붕거리며 말했어요. "근데 경주를 할 상대가 없어서 말야."

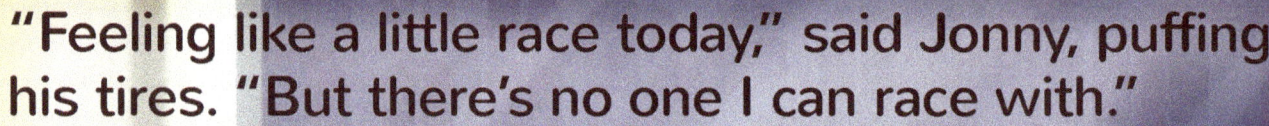

"We can race with you!" said Mike with excitement.
"우리랑 같이하자!" 마이크가 신이 나서 외쳤어요.

"That's what friends are for!" added Scott.
"친구끼리 같이 하면 정말 재밌겠다!" 스캇도 말했어요.

Jonny didn't show much enthusiasm. "Mmm... A champion needs an equal to compete with."
하지만 조니는 시큰둥했어요. "음…챔피언은 그에 걸맞는 상대가 있어야 한다구."

Mike and Scott looked at each other.
마이크와 스캇이 서로를 쳐다보았어요.

"Are we not good?" asked Mike.
"우린 상대가 안되는 거야?" 마이크가 물었어요.

"Oh, you're good," Jonny made a face in the glass window. "But not good enough."
"아냐, 너희도 잘해," 조니가 억지로 웃으며 말했어요. "근데 아주 잘하진 못하잖아."

"Okay, Jonny," said Scott. "We challenge you to a race right now! Let's do Hill Road and see who finishes first."

"좋아, 조니," 스캇이 말했어요. "너에게 도전하겠어! 우리 힐 거리로 나가서 누가 이기는지 한번 해보자."

Jonny considered it with a smirk.

조니는 얼굴을 찌푸린 채 경주를 할지 말지 생각해 보았어요.

As they reached Hill Road, the race began.
조니와 친구들은 힐 거리로 가서, 경주를 시작했어요.

It started with a steep climb. Jonny roared and in seconds was over the incline.
처음에는 가파른 언덕이 나왔어요. 조니는 큰 소리를 내며 단숨에 언덕 위에 다다랐어요.

Mike the bike was already half way... But poor Scott the scooter was huffing and puffing, slowly climbing up.
자전거 마이크는 이제 중간을 오고 있었지만… 불쌍한 킥보드 스캇은 천천히 언덕을 오르며 헉헉대고 있었어요.

Jonny reached the hill and stopped. He looked at the rearview mirror – his friends were far behind.

조니는 언덕 정상에 올라와 멈추었어요. 백미러로 보니 - 친구들이 오려면 아직 한참이나 남아 있었어요.

He was bored. At least the music on the radio was good! He closed his eyes and started moving to the beat.

조니는 지루해졌어요. 다행히 라디오에서 좋아하는 음악이 나왔어요! 조니는 눈을 감고 음악에 맞춰 춤을 추었어요.

Suddenly, something whirred past him. There was only smoke. Mike?

그때 갑자기, 뭔가가 쑹하고 지나가는 느낌이 들었어요. 얼른 보니 연기만 남아있었지 뭐에요. 마이크?

Before he could say a word something else went by. Jonny looked through the disappearing smoke—that was Scott!

뭔가 말을 하기도 전에 또 무언가가 조니를 지나쳐 갔어요. 조니가 사라지는 연기 속을 자세히 살펴보니—그건 바로 스캇이 저 앞에서 달려가는 모습이었어요!

No way! Now he panicked. He should win!

말도 안돼! 조니는 당황스러웠어요. 내가 이길 줄 알았는데!

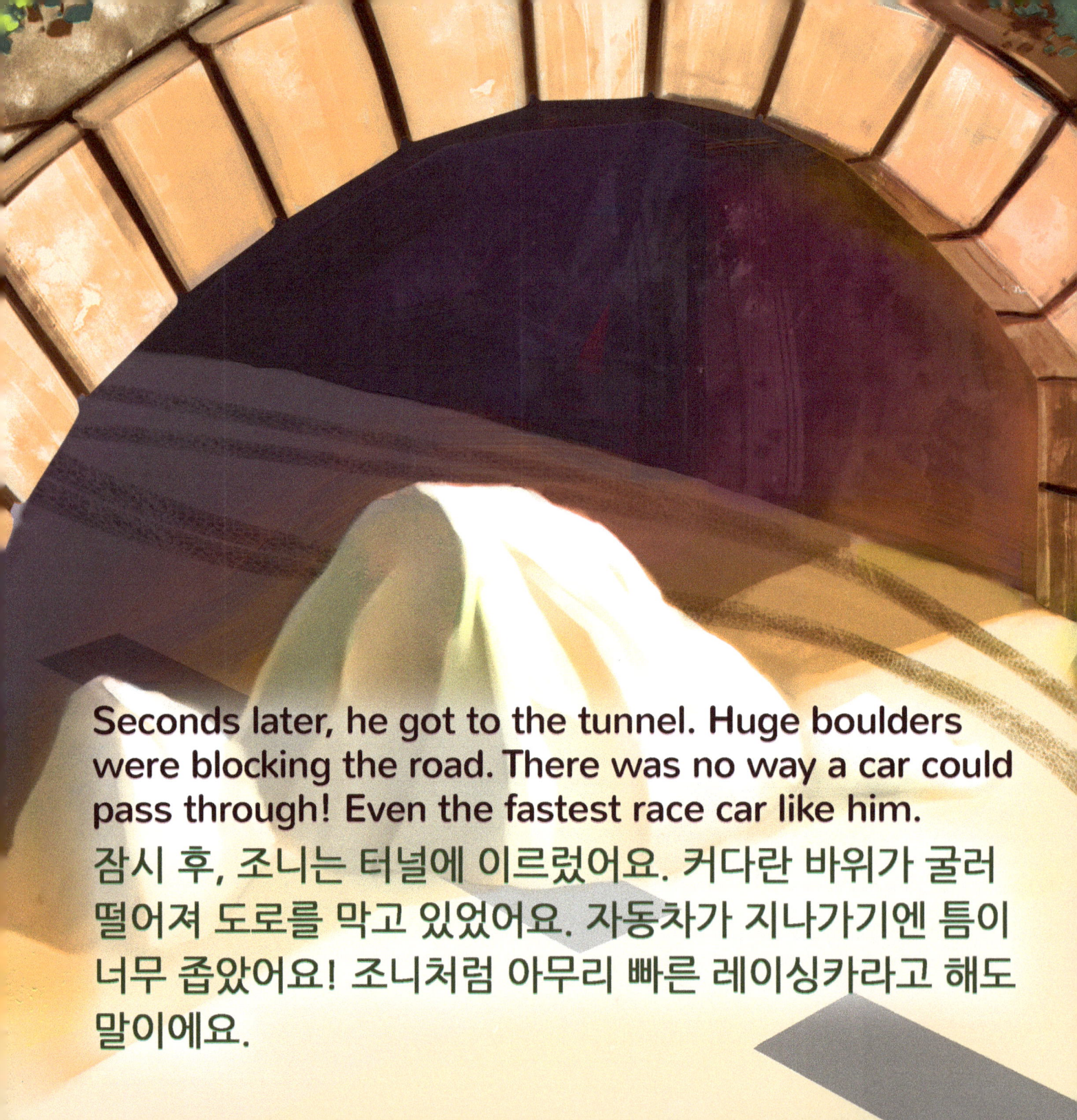

Seconds later, he got to the tunnel. Huge boulders were blocking the road. There was no way a car could pass through! Even the fastest race car like him.

잠시 후, 조니는 터널에 이르렀어요. 커다란 바위가 굴러떨어져 도로를 막고 있었어요. 자동차가 지나가기엔 틈이 너무 좁았어요! 조니처럼 아무리 빠른 레이싱카라고 해도 말이에요.

But then, he saw the tire marks of both Mike and Scott. They had negotiated their way around the stone boulders! Jonny sighed.

하지만 그 때, 돌 사이로 마이크와 스캇의 바퀴 자국이 나 있는 것을 보았어요. 친구들은 그 사이를 지나갈 수 있었던 것이었어요! 조니는 실망스런 한숨을 내쉬었어요.

Meanwhile, Mike came out on the other side of the tunnel. He was leading.

한편, 마이크는 터널을 막 빠져나왔어요. 마이크가 일등을 하고 있었죠.

What kind of a win is that when your friends lose? he thought.

친구들을 지게 만들고 이기는 게 좋은 건가? 마이크는 생각했어요.

In seconds, Scott was next to him.
바로 뒤를 따라, 스캇이 도착했어요.

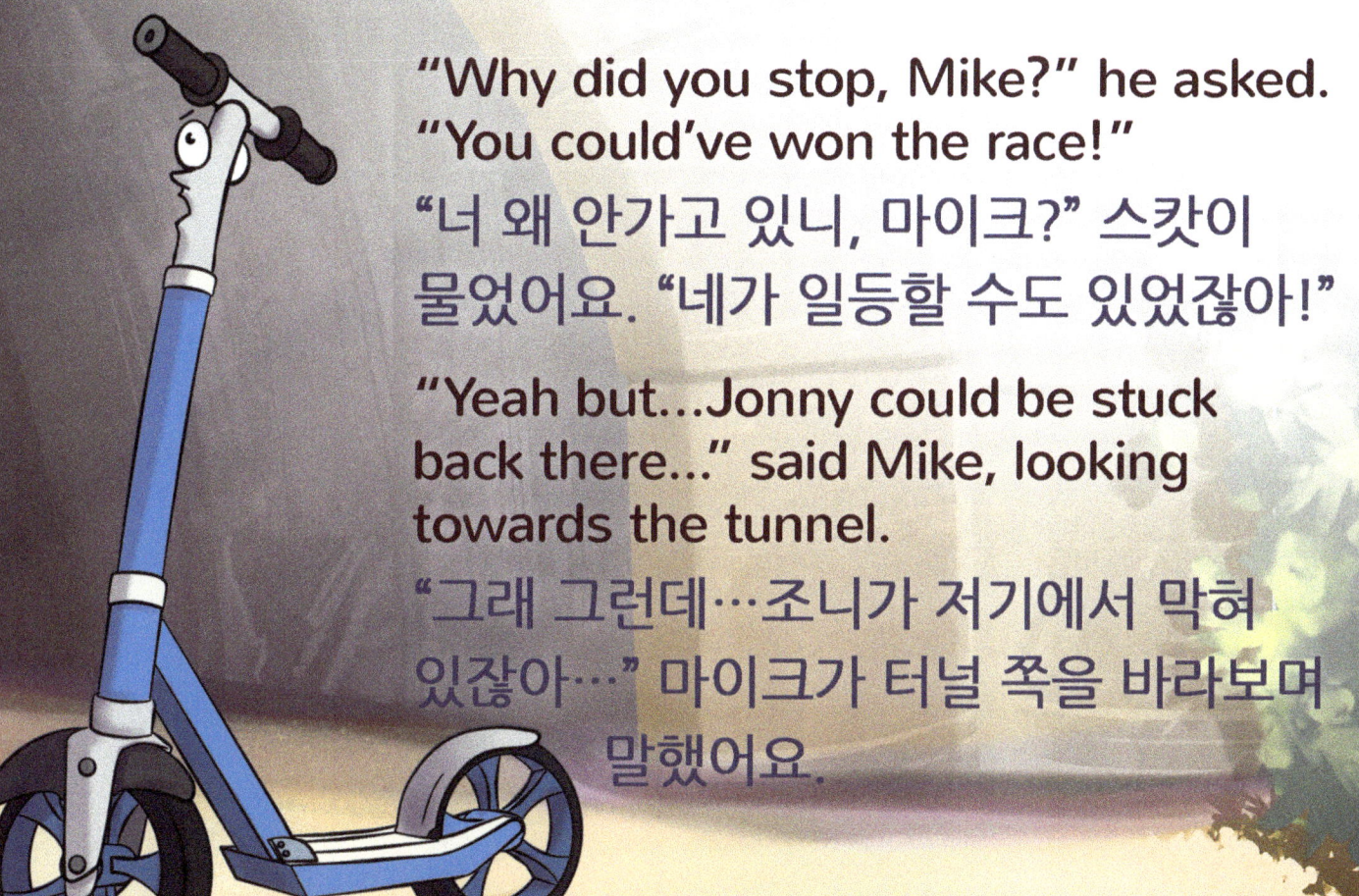

"Why did you stop, Mike?" he asked. "You could've won the race!"

"너 왜 안가고 있니, 마이크?" 스캇이 물었어요. "네가 일등할 수도 있었잖아!"

"Yeah but…Jonny could be stuck back there…" said Mike, looking towards the tunnel.

"그래 그런데…조니가 저기에서 막혀 있잖아…" 마이크가 터널 쪽을 바라보며 말했어요.

A moment of silence passed by.
둘 사이에 잠시 침묵이 흘렀어요.

"Shall we go to check up him?" Scott asked.
"가서 확인해 볼까?" 스캇이 물었어요.

A smile formed on Mike's face. "Let's go!" he yelled and turned back.
마이크의 얼굴에 웃음이 번졌어요. "가자!" 마이크가 소리치고는 터널 안으로 들어갔어요.

At the blocked tunnel, Jonny was sad. Not because he was losing the race but because he was lonely.
막힌 터널 입구에서, 조니는 시무룩하게 앉아 있었어요. 경주에 져서가 아니라 외로웠기 때문이에요.

Suddenly—sound of wheels. Those were Scott and Mike!
그 때—누군가 달려오는 소리가 들렸어요. 그건 바로 스캇과 마이크였어요!

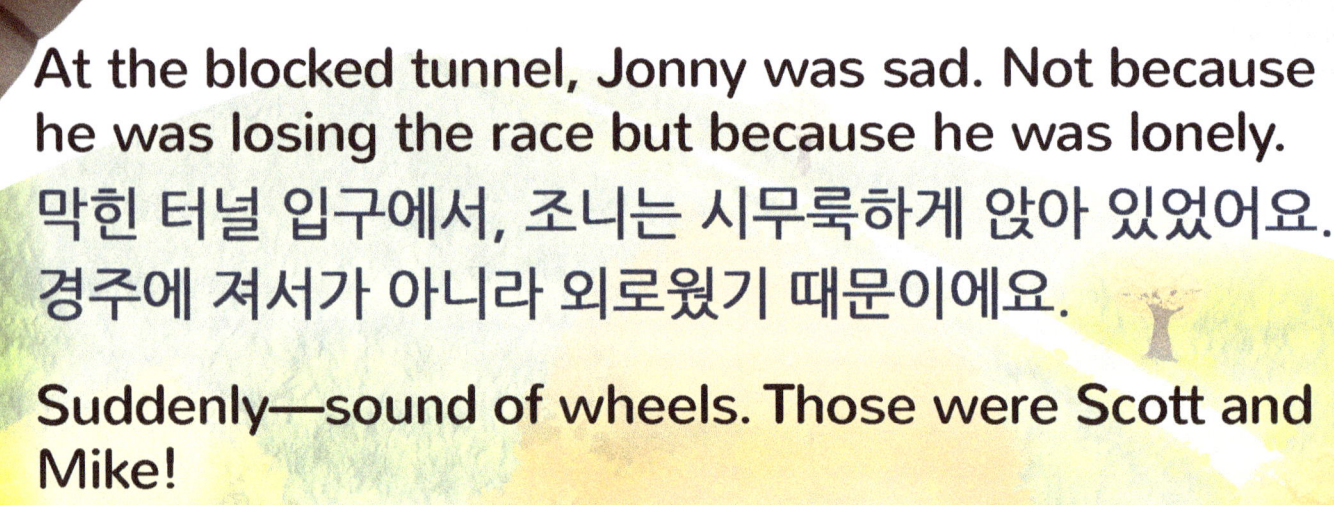

"Mike, Let's move these boulders so Jonny can pass," said Scott.
"마이크, 돌들을 치워서 조니가 통과할 수 있게 해주자," 스캇이 말했어요.

The friends started to work together, pushing the rocks out of the way.
친구들은 힘을 합쳐, 돌들을 밀어내기 시작했어요.

It wasn't easy, but they nudged and nudged and soon there was enough space for Jonny to squeeze through.

쉬운 일은 아니었어요, 하지만 조금씩 조금씩 움직여서 마침내 조니가 지나갈 만한 공간을 만들어 내었어요.

Giggling, they reached the end of Hill Road.
친구들은 함께 웃으며, 힐 거리 끝에 다다랐어요.
"We've won the race—all of us!" exclaimed Mike and Scott.
"우리가 이겼어—모두 다 같이!" 마이크와 스캇이 소리쳤어요.

Only Jonny was quiet. "I behaved badly with you," he admitted. "I realized it late, guys that together we can do much more. Thank you, my friends, for helping me understand that!"

하지만 조니만은 조용했어요. "내가 너희들에게 못되게 군 것 같아," 조니가 말했어요. "늦게서야 깨달았지만, 여럿이 힘을 합치면 더 많은 일을 해낼 수 있다는 걸 알았어. 고마워, 친구들아, 그걸 알게 해줘서 말야!"

Suddenly, there was applause, cheering for this wonderful bunch of three terrific friends.
그 때, 어디선가 박수 소리가 들려왔어요, 마치 이 멋진 세 친구들을 칭찬하듯이 말이에요…

Friends who discovered that none of them was as good as all of them.
친구들은 누가 누구보다 더 잘난 게 아니라 모두가 멋지다는 걸 깨달은 것에 대해 말이죠.

www.ingramcontent.com/pod-product-compliance
Lightning Source LLC
Chambersburg PA
CBHW061145070526
44584CB00033B/4430